BELONGS TO:

LEVI RYSKA

WAPPY 11 !!!

May 12, 2020

Made in the USA
San Bernardino, CA
05 May 2020

70658614R00069